First published 1964
This facsimile published 2010

Beautiful Books Limited
36-38 Glasshouse Street
London W1B 5DL

www.beautiful-books.co.uk

ISBN 9781905636938

9 8 7 6 5 4 3 2 1

This is a facsimile of an historical document first published in 1964.

A catalogue reference for this book is available from
the British Library.

Printed in the UK by TJ International.
www.tjinternational.ltd.uk

Their Trade
is Treachery

Their Trade
is Treachery

---

*. . . I feel it right to warn the
House that hostile intrigue and
espionage are being relentlessly
maintained on a large scale.*

THE PRIME MINISTER, 14TH NOVEMBER 1962

Contents

Illustrations

What it's all about

Spies are with us all the time. They are interested in everything, defence secrets, scientific secrets, political decisions, economic facts; even people's characters – in order to recruit yet more spies.

This booklet tells you about the great hostile spy machine that tries to suborn our citizens and turn them into traitors. It shows you how sometimes it succeeds, and sometime it fails.

This booklet tells you how to recognise at once certain espionage techniques, and how to avoid pitfalls, which could lead to national catastrophe or a personal disaster – or both.

Finally, if you are in possession of information useful to a spy – and that covers a field much wider than you can, perhaps, imagine – or if you are likely to be entrusted with such information, either now or even in the seemingly remote future, this booklet tells you how to foil the spy who will certainly be seeking it.

He may be closer than you think.

Foreword

In this booklet, which is about spies, there are passing references to such well-known names as Fuchs, Blake, Nunn May, Vassall, Houghton, Gee and Lonsdale. Certain aspects of the cases of Petrov and Gouzenko, former Russian intelligence operators, are also examined. In all other case histories described, fictitious names have been used. Apart from the names the stories are true, and have been told to illustrate Iron Curtain Intelligence methods, sometimes subtle, and sometimes crude and brutal.

How the machine was built

Before we watch the machine working, at close hand, let us see how it is constructed, because some understanding of this may give us clues as to how to oppose it.

The basic fact we must face is that the Intelligence Service of the Soviet Union, combined with those of Russia's Communist governed allies, is the biggest machine for the garnering of secret information which the world has ever known.

The Russian, the Eastern European, and the Balkan peoples under the domination, through centuries of conspiracy against automatic regimes, have learnt to combine an aptitude for intrigue with an acquired guile – as have other nations similarly placed. Necessity, born of bitter experience, sometimes fatal experience, has taught them be secretive and secure, patient and unhurried. Furthermore, for reasons of internal security, as well as external spying, the Soviet Intelligence Service has always been regarded by the Russian Government with the same esteem as other countries accord to their armies, navies, and air forces, and has received a commensurate amount of material and moral support.

It is therefore not only large and backed with ample resources; it is able to mix, and to a dangerous degree, what we might call inborn talent with modern experience and methods.

It is a big machine. It is efficient.

If we appear first to concentrate our attention upon the Soviet part of the spy machine rather than upon those of its allies, this is simply because the Soviet Intelligence Service is the main dynamo of the formidable apparatus which is in constant motion against us.

It does not mean that the other parts are to be ignored or despised, as you will read later in these pages; although each of the Iron Curtain countries runs its own Intelligence Service, the Soviet one, as the oldest and most powerful, has lent them aid and training knowledge, and indeed, to a certain extent, continues to direct them, overtly or otherwise.

Fortunately. Although their combined efforts are of menacing proportions, the situation is not hopeless, because like all monster organisations this one has its weak points.

It can be combated by common sense, good will, and a wider knowledge of how it functions.

We will now examine it.

There are two main branches of the Russian Intelligence Service:

1 *The GRU*

This directs military, naval, and air espionage in all foreign countries.

2 *The KGB*

This attends to all the other Intelligence needs of the Soviet Government.

The Intelligence Services of Russia's European Communist allies are organised into somewhat similar branches, and in some measure operate on similar lines.

'Legal' and 'Illegal' Spying

Russian spy networks are of two types. One is the kind which the Russians are pleased to call the 'legal' apparatus.

This network is under the control of a member of the Soviet Embassy staff who is referred to in Russian espionage jargon as The Resident. He enjoys diplomatic immunity. There is, of course, little that is legal about his activities.

So although any British subjects who work for him are liable to imprisonment, the worst that can happen to The Resident is to be declared *persona non grata* – at least until he is called upon, in Moscow, to explain his mistakes.

The Russians call the other spy network, which will have no connection with the Soviet Embassy, the 'illegal' apparatus.

A classic example of an 'illegal' Resident was the spy master who called himself Lonsdale, who directed a network of British traitors, and who was, in fact, a Russian officer posing as a businessman.

The 'illegal' Resident has no connection with any official Russian organisation in the country in which he operates, and no diplomatic immunity. He can be sent to prison, as Lonsdale was.

'Talent spotting'

Before they can obtain the secret information they seek, the enemy Intelligence Services must first find people who can get it, or may be able to get it in the future, and then they must gather personality reports about such people to assess their vulnerability to persuasion or pressure. This process is known as *talent spotting*.

Their victims, willing or otherwise, fall into three categories:

The ideological spy – who thinks the enemy's cause is more just than his own country's, or has other reasons which he thinks good and ethical.

The mercenary spy – who works for money only.

The Spy under pressure – who has been compromised either in Britain, or behind the Iron Curtain, or is an *émigré* with relatives in a Soviet bloc country.

Of all spies, the ideological one is perhaps the hardest to uncover – especially if his conversion to the enemy cause has taken place after he has been given a position of trust.

He may not even be paid and thus perhaps draw attention to himself by spending more than his apparent income – and he may have taken the precaution to keep his conversation quiet.

Such a man was George Blake of the Foreign Office.

If we break down these three categories we will then be able to list the wide range of weapons which are at the disposal of a spy master in his search for recruits.

The Ideological Spy

The ideological spy may work for the overthrow of this country's institutions because he believes that Communism is the best political system for Britain and that only by the downfall of the present ruling class can it be achieved. He is not democratically interested in the fact that the majority of the people may not want such a programme. He knows what is best for them.

The ideological spy may believe that the Western world is plotting war, and think, in some twisted way, that by helping our potential enemies, he will make them so strong that the Western world will be afraid to attack them; or that by supplying them with secret political information he will be enable Russia and her allies to forestall the so-called war plans of Britain and America and thus preserve peace. This is particularly so now that a third of the world is Communist.

The ideological spy may claim that all scientific knowledge, even that involving his country's most vital secrets, should be shared with other countries.

Of such a type was the atom spy, Alan Nunn May, who, with the other scientific spy, Fuchs, received little or no money for his deadly work.

There are indeed no limits to the labyrinthine arguments which an ideological spy may employ to justify his actions. His principal characteristic is intellectual arrogance.

The Mercenary Spy

The mercenary spy is motivated by greed or possibly what, at the beginning of his spy career, he might sometimes tell himself is necessity.

Vassall, the Admiralty spy, claimed that at first he was blackmailed, but later he clearly became a mercenary spy.

Unlike his ideological comrade in treachery, who often receives little or no money, the mercenary spy may call attention to himself because he is a person known to be entrusted with secrets, and because he lives at a standard above his ostensible income.

Ex-Petty Officer Houghton, in the Portland Case, was primarily a mercenary spy. He over-spent, and the fact was noted.

The Spy Under Pressure

The spy under pressure is a person who has been blackmailed. With one possible exception, noted below, he is a person of weak moral fibre, who sinks deeper into the mire because he lacks the courage to face up to the consequences of some past crime or even some mere indiscretion. Rather than do so, he prefers to face far graver consequences in the future.

He may be a man confronted with an accusation of a homosexual act, either true or faked by an enemy Intelligence Service. He may be trying to live down some past dishonesty, or to hide almost anything which he fears be exposed.

The *émigré* is perhaps the one exception mentioned above. He may have to make a terrible choice: to betray the country of his adoption or to expose loved members of his family, still living under Communist rule, to terrible consequences.

Whatever his choice, it might be argued that it could call for a tragic decision which would not be necessarily be rooted in a lack of moral courage.

Whichever way he chooses, and however great his former integrity, he is likely to suffer in the end. If he is a man of honour and sensitivity, his tranquillity of mind is doomed.

The Armoury

We now see the main armoury at the disposal of the spy master:

Ideals – however twisted.

Money and all it will buy.

Fear and all its by-products.

But there is a secondary armoury which must not be forgotten. And we may be sure that the spy master knows how to draw upon it.

Sexual attraction.

Conceit and vanity.

Sense of power – of being part of a strong machine.

Love of intrigue.

Feeling of importance.

Desires for praise and flattery.

A chip on the shoulder.

The weapons are many. The selection of which to use depends upon the assessment of the victim's character, and the observations of the spy master himself.

The Social Approach

When the spy master, either by chance or by cautious machinations, makes a personal contact with a potential agent, he often employs a standard technique which in counter-espionage language is called the social approach.

The pattern of social approaches made over the past twenty years, covering both sexes, all grades of society, and many different occupations, reveals four interesting aspects:

1 The apparently innocent manner in which the first personal contact, if a planned one, is made by the spy master, whether he is 'legal' or 'illegal'; for however much preliminary work may have been done by lesser fry such as talent spotters, this personal contact must be made in the end.

2 Then equally innocent manner in which a 'friendship' is then fostered, without the potential recruit suspecting ulterior motives.

3 The incredible patience employed. Cases are known in which the ostensible 'friendship' has been developed over many years without any further progress being seemingly made. But during this time we can be sure the dossier will have grown thicker as the spy master painstakingly notes his quarry's faults, virtues, changing circumstances, the details of their various meeting places and what was discussed and done, together with copies of the messages which have been sent to Moscow and the instructions received from the spy centre situated in that city.

4 The extraordinarily detailed control often exercised by the Centre over every activity of its spy masters abroad. Although the other Iron Curtain Secret Services have their centres, this is especially true of the Soviet Centre, which has been known to give instructions about the exact place, time, and circumstances when some meeting is to take place far away in London.

These instructions are always carried out to the letter.

The hostile talent spotters range widely. Here are some of the fields in which they are known to have been at work in Australia, not so very long ago:

The Department of External Affairs.

Foreign diplomatic missions.

Menbers of Parliament.

Journalists.

Commercial *aides*.

Scientists.

Counter-espionage and security organisations.

Émigrés circles.

These facts, and many others, are known because a Russian Intelligence Officer, called Petrov, defected in Australia, and a report was subsequently produced by the Australian authorities. The report has a chapter ominously entitled: 'Operations towards setting up an illegal apparatus in Australia.'

The approach at home

Before we come to the more repellent activities of hostile Intelligence Services when operating against British and other nationalities serving behind the Iron Curtain, let us watch exactly how they use the social approach in Britain.

Here are some typical cases.

A Mouse Called Lloyd

This story begins pleasantly enough at a trade reception and ends drearily at an Assize Court.

Given the weak character of the central figure, and the strains and stresses to which he was suddenly submitted, it seems with hindsight that it was almost inevitable that it should have a bad ending.

Yet had he read the signs aright, Lloyd might have been saved.

He didn't, and he was lost. Here is what happened.

The Watchful Colonel

To Colonel Novak, the military attaché, the reception was little different from many others he had attended. It was just one of those occasions when commercial firms meet potential foreign customers. A routine affair. Drink flows. Everybody is friendly. Valuable personal trade contacts can be made, and often are made.

Colonel Novak, outwardly pleasant and relaxed, prowled among the guests, exchanging a handshake here, a few words there. He, too, was seeking valuable personal contacts.

But they were not trade contacts.

Alert and experienced, he began to try to separate the potentially useful people from the obviously useless ones. We do not know what contacts they may have made, but we do know that suddenly, at that reception fraught with much consequence for Britain, Colonel Novak found himself talking to a man called Lloyd.

Colonel Novak saw to it that the talk was a long and cordial one. He had every reason to do so, after he had learnt that Lloyd was an electronics engineer.

When they finally parted and went their separate ways, the electronics engineer called Lloyd had the friendly Colonel's address in his pocket.

More importantly, the friendly Colonel had Lloyd's address.

If Lloyd forgot about Colonel Novak in the ensuing weeks, the Colonel did not forget about Lloyd. In Novak's profession one does not forget about meetings with electronic engineers, even ordinary fellows like Lloyd, and, as Novak was to discover, Lloyd was certainly ordinary. He didn't drink or bet much, or have a mistress, or have homosexual tendencies. In fact, he lived a normal life, with a wife, a good job, and prospects of a happy and honourable retirement.

He was indeed ordinary that even when the telephone rang one day, and he heard the voice of Colonel Novak inviting him and his wife to an Embassy reception, he politely declined.

Perhaps he felt that ordinary people like him and his wife would be socially at a disadvantage in diplomatic circles. Perhaps some inner monitoring voice warned him that acceptance might spell danger. Later, indeed, when he was being interrogated, he claimed, with a pathetic attempt at pompous dignity, that he refused because he 'was not at all sure of the gentleman's status in the country.' Better for Lloyd if the voice had spoken up louder in the years ahead.

Better for Britain, too.

The Hospitable Colonel

Colonel Novak was rebuffed but not defeated. He was a patient man. He was trained to be. Mulling over the notes he had made about his talk with Lloyd, he realised he had been too crude. The social approach covers a multitude of sins and though Lloyd had no apparent sins to exploit, Colonel Novak's notes yielded one important fact.

Lloyd loved music.

Music had been enthusiastically discussed by them both at the trade reception. Music might draw them together again, might form the cement in a long and profitable friendship.

Putting it another way, music might represent the cheese to entice the mouse if not into the trap at least towards it.

More hopeful, now, believing that he had found the right bait, perhaps blaming himself for not thinking of it before, the hospitable Colonel Novak invited Lloyd and his wife to a concert at the Royal Festival Hall, and to supper afterwards.

The offer proved irresistible. Lloyd accepted.

The Patient Colonel

We have mentioned that time means little or nothing to the Russians, and those allies whom they have trained, so it is interesting to see what happened next.

For two long years the grey men at Colonel Novak's particular Centre sat back and watched while the friendship matured between Novak and his wife and Lloyd and Mrs. Lloyd.

They saw how the Lloyds and the Novaks were soon visiting each other's homes, and how the Novaks even attended the reception at the wedding of the Lloyd's eldest daughter and they were content. It so often went this way.

The temptation to act prematurely, to try to learn from Lloyd the secrets he must be able to obtain, would at times have been tremendous. But they did not press. And Novak himself did not put a foot wrong.

All was sweetness and light and music, and a professed desire by the Novaks to compare normal English life with Russian life – as good an excuse as any for a diplomat to put forward when mixing with an electronics engineer in a different station in life.

It might not deceive many people. It should not deceive anybody.

It deceived Lloyd.

Meanwhile the Centre waited. Novak waited. The time was not ripe. But at least the mouse had become used to the cage-trap and was enjoying the cheese. Somewhere, some place, sometime, an opportunity would arise to drop the door. But when?

The chance came in 1957.

Espionage is nothing new. But in recent decades events have revealed that Communist Intelligence services have intensified their efforts to obtain classified information from source in Britain. How many spies are operating in Britain no one can say. But this is known: From 1946 to 1962 eleven persons received prison sentences for offences under the Official Secrets Acts. Photographs of some of the convicted are given on these pages. They present what are ostensibly ordinary harmless people. But their records of treachery stress that at no time can we relax in striving to keep our secrets secret.

Dr. Alan Nunn May, who disclosed secrets relating to atomic energy (10 years).

Another atomic scientist, Dr. Klaus Fuchs, also betrayed his country (14 years).

Because he was an 'illegal' spy master, Conon Molody alias Gordon Lonsdale lacked the protection of diplomatic immunity (25 years), but he was eventually exchanged for Greville Wynne.

Peter and Helen Cohen alias Kroger, sought for years by the F. B. I., who were finally caught in Britain (20 years each).

Harry Houghton and Ethel Gee sold naval secrets (15 years).

John Vassall (above), the Admiralty spy (18 years), and George Blake (below), formerly of the Foreign Office (42 years).

Sometimes spies escape, such as the late Guy Burgess (above) and Donald McLean (below), one-time Foreign Office diplomats, who fled to Russia.

These people fled from the Russians. Armed Soviet agents attempting to take Madame Petrov back to the U. S. S. R. after the defection of her diplomat husband, Vladimir (inset). When their plane refuelled at Darwin, M. Petrov sought political asylum in Australia.

At the end of 1956 Lloyd had joined another electronics firm on the south coast.

The following March his family joined him at the house he had taken in Worthing. It was a disastrous move for all concerned. Domestic troubles arose, swelled, and reached explosion point, and Mrs. Lloyd, no longer able to tolerate the position, left her husband.

Lloyd, worried by debts (increased by the acquisition of a mistress), suffering from terrible strain, encumbered by an aged and senile mother whose continued presence in his house had at least partly caused his domestic troubles, now faced the future – to all intents and purposes alone.

When Colonel Novak heard of these matters, he knew that his time had come. The days of waiting were over.

It was now or never.

The Benevolent Colonel

In the one hand, sympathy and friendship. In the other, money to pay his debts. These were the gifts Colonel Novak offered to the mouse called Lloyd when they dined discreetly in a Soho restaurant a little later.

If Lloyd felt a twinge of alarm at the mention of money, if he suddenly wondered whether, after all, Novak was entirely disinterested – and there is no evidence that he did – the Colonel soon reassured him.

All he wanted were a few catalogues and brochures about electronics in general. That's all. Harmless enough, surely? Almost the sort of thing one friend would do for another without any payment at all.

So, when Colonel Novak suggested they should meet in Brighton in June, Lloyd was willing enough. He had only to come along the coast from Worthing, and a breath of sea air would doubtless be welcome to the Colonel.

He agreed to meet Novak near one of the piers.

Foolish Lloyd. Stupid mouse.

But when Lloyd had handed over his catalogues and brochures at Brighton in June, and when he had opened the envelope Novak gave him, and saw the £50 in it, he must have thought that some friendships pay off better than others.

Perhaps he thought Novak's next proposed meeting place, a crossroad near Worthing, a little odd, even if convenient. If he did, he crushed the thought. He agreed to the meeting.

The cage-door was closing fast.

It closed completely after the meeting at the crossroads. Novak said the catalogues were not quite what he wanted. He stressed his interest in radar. Significantly, he omitted doing one thing which he had done at the previous meeting. He handed over no more money.

Significantly, too, he again suggested a road junction for the next meeting.

Now was literally the moment of truth.

Even Lloyd could no longer persuade himself that the benevolent Colonel Novak was prepared to trade good money for mere catalogues.

Now was the last chance to draw back from the edge of the espionage trap. Others had done so before him, and others would do so after him. Not so Lloyd. He agreed to the meeting, and all that that implied.

With his eyes wide open to what he was doing, he crossed the threshold of the cage for the last time, and the trap closed behind him. Henceforth he was the prisoner of a hostile Intelligence Service. A willing prisoner. They never had to blackmail him.

The social approach had lured him: a taste for money had trapped him. He was now a traitor selling his country's secrets for cash. It had become as simple as that.

The money was useful and he could always do with more of it.

From this time onwards his descent was rapid.

He had every right to go to a cupboard where secret blueprints were kept. So meetings were planned for week-ends, because at Lloyd's place of employment some of the staff worked on Saturday mornings.

On Saturday mornings, Lloyd extracted material.

On Saturday afternoons, he gave it to the Colonel Novak.

On Sundays, Novak gave it back, having photographed it.

Secret ways were evolved to inform Lloyd of the place, date, and time of meetings and now Novak showed an interest in things other than radar. To Lloyd the payments seemed good.

In October 1957, Lloyd received £50.

In December, it was £100.

In January 1958, it was £50.

In February, it was £200.

End of The Road

But now events took a curious shape. At the February meeting, the documents were not returned by Novak, but by a deputy, who said Novak was sick. A further meeting with Novak was nevertheless arranged for 29th March 1958.

Lloyd waited in vain.

Colonel Novak did not arrive. Colonel Novak's deputy did not arrive. Perhaps the Colonel sensed he was under suspicion.

Perhaps the unusually large sum of £200 was a farewell gift of cash to a man who would certainly need it in the future. Not that there was much future left now.

Lloyd was never met again by his spy master or even his deputy.

Instead in May 1958, at a time and place of their own choosing, he was met by a different set of people, arrested, put on trial at the Assize Court, and sentenced to fourteen years imprisonment.

Poor, silly, treacherous Lloyd.

After his sentence, he thought he had been harshly treated. Some idea of his twisted thinking can be seen from the following incident.

At one stage, Novak proposed 'a dead letter box', a hiding place where documents could be concealed, collected by Novak, and later recovered by Lloyd. Lloyd refused to co-operate. He said he thought it was 'underhand'.

The Reasons Why

He fell because he did not recognise the social approach when it happened; because he did not honestly ask himself whether it was likely a diplomat like Colonel Novak would need to mix with Lloyd's family to learn of English ways; because in his straits he could not resist money; and because Novak played gently with him, at first whetting his appetite for money by paying a lump sum in exchange for innocuous catalogues.

And it all began with a trade reception – and a talk about music.

The name of the man was Lloyd, but it might have been Brown, or Smith, or Jones, or any man or woman who does not understand the social approach, or appreciate that big diplomatic cats do not normally play with humble mice without good reason and a hope of profit.

Who's For Tennis?

Sometimes hostile Intelligence Services employ unorthodox recruiting methods of a kind which at first sight have a startling hit-or-miss appearance. The danger of such methods lies in the very fact that they seem so divorced from calculated Secret Service machinations. Their slapdash appearance gives them a spurious aura of innocence.

The story of a young clerk, James Howard, provides an illustration of this.

Howard worked for a time in the West Country.

Shortly before he was due to transfer to London, young Howard was idly reading the paper when he noticed a somewhat unusual advertisement. It had apparently been inserted by a foreigner living in London who was anxious to meet a young Englishman with a view to playing tennis.

Howard liked foreigners. He found them often more free and easy than his own countrymen. He replied – and in return received a letter from an address in Cadogan Gardens, London, as a result of which, a week before he was due to be transferred, Howard, the clerk, found himself being entertained in a local hotel by an Iron Curtain diplomat and his wife.

The diplomat was called Vasek.

Howard was discreetly questioned during the meal about his background, relatives, and education. When the evening was over, the diplomat Vasek knew for certain that Howard was a man whom it was worth-while to cultivate.

He was employed in a civilian capacity in an establishment connected with a department of the Armed Forces. He may have only been a clerk, but in Vasek's eyes he was a clerk with a difference.

So, on 4th December 1957, the unusual 'friendship' began, with it's inevitable round of discreet dinners, visits to the cinema and theatre – and tennis or plans for tennis when the weather permitted.

But on this occasion Vasek had a short run.

On the 12th March 1958, Vasek and his wife were observed to leave home by car. More important, they were taking measures which were obviously intended to elude anybody who might be trying to follow them.

They did not succeed.

At the Bond Street Underground Station, the security men saw Vasek meet a young man, take him to the cinema, then to dinner in Chelsea, and then to his home in West London. The next morning James Howard was followed to work.

Now the security machinery got to work on a broad front. The following steps were taken:

1 Consultation with Howard's department revealed him to be a clerical officer, aged 23, who would not normally himself handle secret material, but whose duties allowed him into rooms where such material was handled by others.

2 A number of friends were discreetly investigated. They appeared to be of no security interest, though Howard later admitted that, as he put it, they were 'unorthodox from the point of view of sex'.

3 Observation was naturally continued on Howard himself. On 15th April, he was seen to visit Vasek's home carrying a well-filled briefcase – a briefcase which he had carried on previous occasions.

4 Finally, in this particular case, it was decided prevention was better than cure – and possible punishment. Howard was interviewed, the social approach technique was explained, and he promised to see no more of Vasek.

In the event, Howard did not keep his promise. The social entertainment proved too strong an attraction.

But now, ironically, Vasek became almost as disillusioned

with Howard as the security authorities. Here is what happened.

At one stage Howard had told Vasek that he was bored with his job and underpaid. Vasek alarmed at future prospects – or perhaps lack of them – urged him to be patient. But by June, Howard had left Crown employment and taken a job in commerce. This was bad, from Vasek's point of view.

Worse was the fact that Howard did not tell him.

Vasek only found out by chance and from now on he regarded Howard as useless and unreliable investment. Slowly and tactfully he began to disengage himself from this unprofitable, time-wasting, and irritating venture.

James Howard's whirl in diplomatic circles was over.

How Conceit Works
No harm, as far is known, was done to national interests, but the case is of note for the following reasons:

(a) Vasek, with his advertisement, flung his not very attractive bait into a wide sea – and got a bite of the kind he wished.

(b) Howard, when questioned, admitted he had seen a written instruction to report to his employers any contacts with Iron Curtain officials.

(c) He considered it 'a piece of monstrous impertinence, the worst type of bureaucratic nonsense'.

(d) He said he knew Vasek to be 'as straight as a die'.

(e) He considered he was capable of looking after himself.

(f) He clearly was not capable of looking after himself. Given half a chance, he would doubtless have fallen into the first real trap Vasek set for him, homosexual or otherwise.

(g) He must, at the very least, have had certain suspicions about Vasek's interests and ultimate intentions, since he tried to deceive him when he left Crown service. He wanted, in fact, a few of the lesser fruits of espionage without the risks of spying.

(h) He thought he could in some measure double-cross an experienced hostile Intelligence officer.

James Howard was wrong all along the line.

It may be unnecessary to add that Vasek said that one reason for getting to know Howard was to learn about the British way of life with the aid of ordinary British people: the voice was the voice of Vasek, but the thread bare old excuse recalls that of his superior officer – none other than the patient Colonel Novak, of the Lloyd case, whom we have already watched at work.

So far it has been music and tennis. In the next story it is football.

Nikolai Kicks Off

Nikolai was the genuine article, which in these pages means that he was a Russian Intelligence Officer.

This implies, in turn, that every time he met somebody abroad he asked himself, 'Can this person help me? If so, how can I get to know him better, and make him work for me?'

One September evening, Nikolai went into a public house in the Shepherd's Bush district, London. In an ingenious sort of way he asked a man drinking by himself what he, as a foreigner, should order.

We do not know, and never will know, whether Nikolai approached the stranger as a result of some talent-spotting operation, or whether, on the principle that one has to start somewhere, he was employing hit-or-miss tactics. If the latter, he was very lucky indeed.

The stranger was Sergeant Brown, an Army clerk working in the War Office.

We may as well say at once that when he had given his own name to the sergeant, Nikolai expressed a keen desire to understand the British way of life and how ordinary people spent their leisure.

However much the security authorities may have heard of this worthy and apparently widespread desire among Iron Curtain diplomatic staff, it sounded reasonable enough to the simple sergeant, who chatted away happily and mentioned, among other things, that he played for the War Office football team.

Nikolai may or may not have been interested in sport, in general, or football in particular. If he wasn't, he clearly had to be.

In the fullness of time, Nikolai, officer of the Russian Intelligence Service, became a firm supporter of the British War Office football team.

It was a promising kick-off.

Nikolai Wins Friends

Nikolai, interpreter and clerk in the office of the Soviet Military Attaché, became quite popular with the team, especially with White, the Captain, and Green, the secretary, who were civilian clerical officers.

He became even more popular in November when he contributed the drinks, including the inevitable bottle of vodka, at a party given at his suggestion in the flat of Sergeant Brown, and during the following months Nikolai industriously cemented his relationship with his little network of clerks.

He met them separately at agreed meeting places, such as Trafalgar Square. He entertained them individually to dinner and a cinema or theatre show. He gave them presents of gin and cigarettes.

On one occasion there was a hint of money in the air. He told the team captain, White, that he was collecting material for an innocuous article he was writing for a Soviet journal, and invited White to assist him. Further, he not only promised White a fee, but offered to give it to him an advance.

The game was going well, in Nikolai's opinion.

There was only one thing wrong.

At the November party, a certain War Office staff sergeant thought it well to make a report of it, even though it seemed to be merely a pleasant, cheerful evening.

As a result Sergeant Brown was interviewed. So was team captain White. They were warned of danger, told they could continue seeing Nikolai, but instructed to report any significant moves.

So quite soon after the kick-off Nikolai was off-side – though he didn't know it.

The danger had been contained through the sound common sense of a staff sergeant who reported contact with a Russian official, even though – as James Howard had at first thought – the social relationship seemed harmless.

24

But there is no doubt that in the beginning the three clerks were amused and flattered and entertained by Nikolai's attention.

Of interest, too, is the incident of collecting material for a harmless article. This hoary old approach, leading to possible sinister inveiglement, is almost as frequent as the so-called desire to get to know the British way of life by mixing with 'ordinary people'.

Both tactics can lead to disaster. Both are easy to discern.

We will now briefly observe a more delicate approach.

Miss Benson Regrets
In this very short story there are only two characters – and a lady's ring. But it shows an original and elastic mind at work.

Krasnov, an official at the London embassy of one of Russia's allies, was good-looking and pleasant. He spoke excellent English.

He was well fitted for the role he had to fill.

His target: Miss Benson, secretary of a Member of Parliament.

His reason: she might see documents summarising Western views on certain current political issues.

He had met her in the course of the social life which forms part of all political and diplomatic activity, and it may well be that he really liked Miss Benson. In view of Krasnov's attractive personality, it would certainly not be surprising if Miss Benson liked Krasnov.

Be that as it may, in the fullness of time a friendship developed between them, and in the fullness of time, too, the Member of Parliament went abroad for a while, leaving Miss Benson looking after his affairs.

It is interesting and instructive to watch how from now on this man and this woman, who may well have been good friends, put personal considerations aside and reacted each according to the basic demands of the duties they were carrying out and the common sense they both possessed.

For Krasnov, the absence of the Member of Parliament was a golden opportunity. It was his big chance.

One day he casually remarked that Members of Parliament must surely be interested and well informed on topical, political matters. He, too, was interested in such matters. Surely Miss Benson must have a chance to see documents on this subject?

Miss Benson discreetly replied that it was almost impossible for her to obtain such documents.

For Krasnov this was discouraging; but he did not consider the position hopeless. After all, Miss Benson had, perhaps deliberately, in his view, used the word 'almost'.

Krasnov was now faced with a problem. As an intelligent man, he had rightly judged that a crude offer of money, as an opening gambit, would be worse than useless to a person of Miss Benson's character.

He solved the problem to his own satisfaction by seeking Miss Benson's advice in the little matter of choosing a ring to send home as a present to his wife.

Miss Benson was not particularly surprised when she herself received a ring worth about £20 a few days later.

Neither were the security authorities surprised, to whom she had by now, with common sense and acumen, reported all the circumstances.

Miss Benson returned the ring, expressing her polite regrets that it was impossible, in her position, to accept a gift.

Thus the affair began and ended with delicacy and good manners on both sides, and the courtesies were at all times maintained.

For Krasnov, the return of the ring was the end, if not of a long and beautiful friendship, at least of a short and hopeful one.

They did not meet again.

The Russians have a phrase for incidents such as these: *The scythe has struck a stone.*

The Lonely Dutchman

There was nothing at all delicate, at least at one stage, in the methods used to suborn George Reynolds, a 19-year-old

National Service member of the Royal Air Force, as will be shown in this story.

The enemy Intelligence Services spend much time and money talent-spotting among those serving with the British Armed Forces. We have already seen Nikolai at work with the three War Office clerks. Here is a case in which an RAF man was involved.

George Reynold's time came one Sunday in May 1957.

Reynold's duties in the RAF were those of a tape relay operator, passing messages both in code and plain language, but on the Sunday in question he was on leave.

Wearing his RAF uniform, no doubt partly because it is easier to get a lift in a uniform, he was patiently waiting by the roadside until a car should stop and help him on his way to London from his station at Newmarket.

In London, his wife waited, little knowing that, when a car did stop, it would involve her husband in trouble of which she herself would have no inkling.

Come to that, Reynolds didn't know it himself, of course – not at first, and by the time he did know it, it was too late for one of his weak character.

Yet had anybody asked Reynolds, that morning in May, whether he was capable of 'looking after himself', there is no doubt that, like James Howard, he would have indignantly answered in the affirmative.

Certainly there was nothing suspicious, at least to Reynolds, about the friendly Dutchman who stopped for him.

What could be more harmless than a Dutch commercial salesman, calling himself Marek, a man who in the general exchange of chat about jobs said that he himself was, in a sense, interested in transmissions, since he sold radios and tele-printer? A bond in common, so to speak.

Furthermore, the Dutchman said he was lonely. He had few friends in England, poor chap. So when Marek suggested that Reynolds and his wife might like to dine with him in London, it seemed almost a kindness to accept. If not a kindness, at least it would be a free meal.

The only trouble was:

(a) Marek was not a Dutchman.

(b) Marek was not a salesman.

(c) Marek was certainly not lonely. He was an Iron Curtain diplomat and spy, had many acquaintances, and the full power of a hostile Intelligence Service to call on.

Temporary Dividends

In the event, Reynolds and his wife had quite a few free meals – about five or six, by the end of July 1957.

Marek even made George Reynolds a member of a London club, and, what is more, paid his subscription for him.

Marek also gave the Reynolds a television set. It was a used one. This might have been subtlety, on the grounds that a new set might seem a bit too much of a good thing, whereas a used set, from a man in the business, could be understandable. On the other hand, we must face the fact that it might have been just a prudent measure of economy.

Still, for Reynolds the business of helping a lonely Dutchman was paying good dividends, one way and another.

The crunch was bound to come.

The first hint of it occurred at a lunch between Marek and Reynolds, by themselves, in August.

Here the usual old gambit of offering money in exchange for harmless catalogues and brochures was cleverly and surprisingly reversed.

Marek *had* the literature: but he claimed he couldn't *understand* it.

Neither, as it happened, could Reynolds; nor, Reynolds pointed out, did they have a technical reference library at his unit headquarters.

This was only a momentary setback for Marek. Indeed, in view of his long-term plans it was hardly a setback at all, because unfortunately Reynolds now had a bright idea.

He remembered he had at home some notebooks dating from the time of his RAF training. Anxious, in some way, to repay his lonely but generous Dutch friend, he promised to lend the notebooks to Marek some time.

Then, accompanied by his wife, Reynolds went happily on holiday.

The Grateful Victim
Marek was happy, too. He had reason to be.

His hospitality and gifts had clearly created in Reynolds a sense of obligation which could lead to a rosy future.

These initial tactics, these preliminary steps of making a potential victim feel grateful, were well known to Marek, the spy. They often bought fine results in the end. They might succeed now.

They did.

They succeeded so well that on his return, refreshed from his holiday, possibly eager to help his good friend Marek, and almost certainly eager for some more free meals, Reynolds went so far as to search diligently for Marek at various drinking clubs until he found him.

So Marek didn't need to chase Reynolds now. Reynolds was chasing him. His victim was running towards him, and eagerly, too.

However, when he invited Reynolds and his wife out to dinner again, and arranged to pick them up by car. He did casually remind Reynolds about the technical notebooks.

After all, one might as well make sure about things.

In the car that evening the two wives sat behind, the two men in front. In the car, Reynolds discreetly slipped the notebooks on to the shelf beneath the dashboard. It was furtive action, the first of many to come.

His wife did not see it. She was not meant to see it.

Often in the spy battle it is innocent wives who suffer most when their husbands become creatures of the spy masters.

In early September Marek decided that the time had come for the pay-off to begin in earnest. He had told Reynolds that he would return the notebooks to him in Newmarket, and in Newmarket he duly entertained Reynolds to dinner and drinks at an inn.

But he returned no notebooks.

Instead, he suggested that they might drive to Epping Forest and have a quiet talk, and there, in a quiet clearing in the forest, a dramatic little scene took place.

The lonely Dutchman dropped his disguise.

He asked Reynolds point blank to collaborate with him in obtaining secret information.

Reynolds refused.

Marek was ready for this. He pointed out, no doubt in as nice a way as possible, that by handing over his notebooks Reynolds had placed himself in what could be called a difficult position. It was naked blackmail now.

Marek added, perhaps to discourage any ideas of violence, that in fact the notebooks were hidden somewhere else in the forest. So they were.

In the event, Marek returned them. There was no reason why he shouldn't. As he pointed out ominously to Reynolds, he was retaining photographic copies of them.

He gave Reynolds £1 for his taxi fare back to London. The airman went by Underground and kept the change.

Reynolds had pleaded for a period in which to think it over. He had made up his mind by the time they met again, this time in Clapham.

He agreed. He was hooked.

From now on, the case assumed a familiar pattern, at least in some respects.

Clandestine methods of communication were employed so that when Reynolds wished for a meeting he was to make a mark against the letter A in a telephone kiosk.

A dead letter box was arranged where Reynolds could leave material of possible interest to Marek; and again the telephone directory was to indicate the time and date when the material would be there.

In return for his traffic in treason Reynolds received several hundred pounds. One payment was for as much as £150, in one pound notes, to enable Reynolds to make a deposit on a flat.

Indeed, compared to the value of the information supplied by Lloyd, the electronics engineer, and Lloyds potentialities. Reynolds was well rewarded for his treachery.

He would doubtless have been even better rewarded had he agreed to stay in the RAF when his National Service was finished.

As an earnest of better things, Marek offered him £300 down if he would stay on.

But Reynolds refused absolutely.

He had had several hundred pounds, a deposit on a flat, a great deal of hospitality – and a used television set. Perhaps he thought that enough was as good as a feast, at least in RAF sphere.

Marek discussed with him various possibilities in civilian W/T communication, where he might continue his secret activities, but it is perhaps significant that the next time they met was the last. It was on 2nd May 1958, and Reynolds's service in the RAF was finished.

At this meeting, Marek said that his own period of service in Britain – was also coming to an end.

He went through the motions, at least, of arranging how his successor would get in touch with Reynolds, if he so wished:

(a) Reynolds would receive a post card from a person with a fictitious name. The postcard would be posted in Paris.

(b) Reynolds would then suggest a time and date for a meeting, in a telephone directory.

(c) Subsequently, he would walk round a block of buildings, be approached by a stranger, and mutual identifications would be established by an innocent question and answer, which Marek then gave him.

It appears that no post card ever came from Paris.

Possibly the arrangements were made in earnest. Possibly, too, Marek, or his successor, having discussed matters with their Centre, decided that Reynolds had outlived his usefulness and should be tactfully discarded.

As far as the security authorities were concerned, Reynolds had certainly outlived his usefulness.

He naturally thought that he had escaped observation.

He was wrong.

He had been under investigation for some months. Early in 1959, the case having progressed no further, he was interrogated.

Marek had foreseen this possibility. At their last meeting he had warned Reynolds what to do if it happened:

(a) He should readily admit friendship.

(b) He should steadily deny passing information.

So perhaps there was a third possible reason why no post card came from Paris. Maybe Marek thought the authorities were suspicious.

At his interrogation, Reynolds at first adhered strictly to Marek's instructions. But at length he told the truth, and it was possible to fill in the details of the story of 'Marek, the Lonely Dutchman'.

The approach from abroad

Hostages of fate, a hackneyed enough title, is unfortunately exactly appropriate to a threat already mentioned earlier in these pages.

The threat is based upon a heartless exploitation of human love and affection, It has its roots in distant lands but its tentacles reach unwillingly both for our secrets and for other information.

The word 'unwilling' is used because in most cases it probably represents the true state of mind of the *émigrés* who are involved.

The *émigrés* concerned are usually people who have left their homeland because they would not tolerate life under a Communist Government. Clearly, they would not normally wish to help that Government.

Sometimes they feel they must.

The compulsion stems from the relatives they have left behind, the hostages from whom they have been separated by fate in the shape of world affairs.

One day a man may come to them and say: 'Unless you do what I wish, unless you spy for me, things could go badly for your relations – and you know what that means.'

The blackmail is hard to resist.

The Hidden Risks

The dangers of this type of *émigré* are as follows:

(a) The fact that true political *émigrés* inevitably, and rightly, arouse in us a certain feeling of sympathy.

(b) Some of them may arouse personal recollections of the time when they or their compatriots were comrades in arms.

(c) Since they have fled from Communism, or declined to return to their own Communist-ruled country, with all that that implies in the way of exile, there is an indication to think they must be 'all right' from the security angle.

And so most of them are.

Reluctantly, however, it is necessary to regard with great caution every *émigré* who still has relatives in Russia or in the lands of her Communist allies

In protecting ourselves we are ultimately protecting the *émigrés* and their relatives.

Sometimes the *émigré* is used to try to gain information about State secrets, but sometimes he can be used in quite a different capacity, as the following two little stories show.

In order to understand what is behind them, it is necessary to appreciate that every *émigrés* from a Communist regime is a very bad advertisement for Communism indeed.

Many *émigrés*, especially Russians, have strong emotional ties with the mother country. To sever them rather than live under Communism represents a slap in the face to which Communist Governments are even more sensitive than they are about most things, which is saying a good deal.

Such Governments take an unhealthy interest in their *émigrés* – unhealthy, that is, for the *émigrés* – and try to learn as much as possible about them.

If they can entice them to renounce life under a Western democracy and return home, so much the better.

They also regard them, sometimes with reason, as centres of intrigue and anti-Communist propaganda. In short:

(a) Communist Governments don't like *émigrés*.

(b) Communist Governments want to know all about them – and take steps to find out.

The Lost Sheep

A convenient stepping-stone in such matters for the Rumanian Government, in the opinion of Mr. Andreas, the diplomat and Intelligence Officer, was a certain Mrs. Mayfield, of his nationality but wife of a British subject.

She was convenient for three reasons:

1 She had an old mother at home.

2 She wanted to bring her old mother to England, which necessitated an exit visa.

3 She had worked at one time for the Foreign Office and the

BBC, and knew quite a number of *émigrés* from her own country.

The chance was not one to be missed.

One day, after she had duly applied for an exit visa for her mother, Mrs. Mayfield, much to her surprise, found Mr. Andreas from the legation on her doorstep.

Mr. Andreas seemed in affable and helpful mood.

He said that pending the possible grant of an exit visa for the old mother, Mr. and Mrs. Mayfield might like to visit her; in which case he, benevolent Mr. Andreas, could help with visas for them; or they might care to send her parcels of certain commodities which she could sell on the Black Market and thereby improve her living conditions.

All he wanted in return was a flow of information about *émigrés* in Britain.

Mrs. Mayfield declined to help.

When it was pointed out by Andreas, no longer so affable, that her obstinancy might have the most unfavourable consequences for her mother, Mrs. Mayfield's personal dilemma must have been acute and painful. Perhaps she had always expected such a day to arrive, perhaps she had long since decided upon her attitude in the face of such blackmail.

She remained firm.

In this case, the story has a happy ending. Mrs. Mayfield's courageous defiance cost her nothing.

Her mother obtained her exit visa and came to England – though not, one may be sure, as a result of any helpful action by the frustrated Mr. Andreas.

The probable explanation is that Andreas heard of the visa application through is official position, and decided upon a personal ploy, an off-the-cuff blackmail action which, eventually, had only one result for him: he was declared *persona non grata*.

But had Mrs. Mayfield's mother received parcels, sold the contents on the Black Market, and been arrested, the pressure could perhaps have become almost unbearable, even for Mrs. Mayfield.

Black Market blackmail is not uncommon and features in a

later story, but first we will glance at some activity among Russians *émigrés*.

More Lost Sheep

In the autumn of 1955, the Soviet Government surprised the world by declaring an amnesty for all categories of political refugees except those against whom war crimes could be proved.

This superficially broadminded gesture was not, of course, grounded in humanitarianism, but was designed to lure back to Russia those groups of refugees whose continued residence abroad was, at least, a source of political embarrassment to the Soviet Government.

A result of the amnesty was that the Russian Consular authorities tried to learn even more than usual about their *émigrés*, both as groups and as individuals.

Here is an example of the sort of thing that happened.

One day, in 1956, a Soviet Consular Clerk arrived in this country. His duties seemed innocuous. They were concerned with travel bookings, and arrangements to supply visas, for Embassy and Trade Delegation officials and for people wishing to visit Russia. He also had to supervise the arrivals and departures of Russian ships from the Port of London and maintain contact with British shipping agents.

He had, however, another duty, which did not become immediately apparent.

It became apparent when one day a frightened Baltic refugee called Jonas Vilnis sought the help of the British police.

Jonas Vilnis had an interesting tale to tell.

As in the case of Mrs. Mayfield, Vilnis had had a caller. But whereas Mrs. Mayfield's caller had been from a satellite legation, this visitor said he was from the Soviet Foreign Office itself.

It was the Consular Clerk, using a false name – and armed with a letter from a friend of Vilnis who was still in the Soviet Union.

The Consular Clerk wanted four things.

1 Information about fellow *émigrés*.
2 Names and addresses of subscribers to the particular *émigré* newspaper in which Vilnis was interested.
3 Names and addresses of other Balts in this country to whom the Embassy could send copies of a Russian paper printed in their own particular language.
4 Name and address of somebody who might be willing to return to his homeland, and later re-enter Britain, allegedly to make propaganda.

Under one guise or another, and for whatever purpose, revealed or unrevealed, the demands mostly boiled down to an operation with a single aim – to obtain information about *émigrés'* groups and personalities in this country.

Jonas Vilnis declined to assist and, as stated went to the police. It was the only right and sensible thing to do.

It soon became apparent that blatant bullying, and the grossest intimidations, were being employed by certain Russian officials. This was not only intolerable to public opinion but also against the laws of this country. The Russians were officially warned that further actions of this kind would not be permitted. The activities ceased – at least openly.

Such crude methods as those employed by the Russians and their allies are far more removed from their normal subtlety, and can hardly be regarded as intelligence work.

But they illustrate that, though they may think themselves secure, political refugees are never quite beyond the reach of their Governments.

Under extreme pressure from abroad only the bravest can be defiant.

Stalking The Duck
Before we leave this subject, however, it is worthwhile to note how hostile Intelligence Services can employ exactly opposite methods to those described above – no threats or blackmail, that is, but the technique of The Lure. Here is how it can work.

In this case, Vladislav Gorski, the Polish civilian barber, began it all, though in an innocent enough way – he happened to be employed at an RAF station near Bath.

Gorski was a curious mixture, in that although an *émigré* he had chosen to retain his Polish nationality. He was, therefore, not perhaps an ideal choice, on form, for a job at an RAF base, but if the Polish Intelligence Service ever had any vague ideas of coercing the humble hairdresser they soon had more important prey in sight.

Gorski became a mere stepping-stone to more ambitious plans.

He inadvertently became a stepping-stone when, in the fullness of time, he applied to the Polish Embassy for a passport to visit his son in Poland, and arrange, if possible, for the young man to join him in England.

The passport, perhaps to Gorski's surprise, was granted.

Doubtless one fact had escaped his attention: when applying for a passport he had been obliged to state where he was employed.

Nevertheless, nothing happened to Gorski, the barber, when he went to Poland, and in due course he happily returned to his barbering.

Then one day he received a visit, and the visitor, calling ostensibly for social purposes, was none other than an official who had interviewed him at the Consulate-General.

He was also, as it happened, a member of the Polish Intelligence Service.

Now luck played a part, or so it must have seemed to the Polish Intelligence Service. For Gorski, by chance, was at the time entertaining another Pole. The other Pole was called Zaremba. Whatever ideas the UB man may have had about Gorski, he must have speedily changed them.

It is not surprising.

Zaremba was a warrant officer attached to Fighter Command and had full knowledge of highly secret radar equipment.

Zaremba became the prey now.

The Sitting Duck

Nothing happened for some months. Doubtless it took time not only to evolve the plot but to get it approved by the Polish Centre. These things are not hurried.

Like all good plans the one chosen was a simple one, though but for another stroke of luck it might have required a long period to mature.

It began with a further visit to Gorski, but on this occasion by two officers of the military branch of the Polish Intelligence Service. Ostensibly, the visit was a social one, and if the simple barber was flattered it was only because he omitted to ask himself what he had to offer, apart perhaps from a free hair-cut, to two Embassy officials.

What he had to offer was an introduction, some day, to Warrant Officer Zaremba.

This might have been long delayed, of course, had it not been for the fortunate coincidence that Zaremba was also visiting Gorski when the two officers called.

The bird was waiting on the premises.

The Polish Intelligence Service was in no hurry. Zaremba must not be made suspicious. Any instinctive hostility had to be overcome.

He had to be persuaded that Poland, even under Communism, was changing, growing more tolerant and liberal-minded, that even Communists, these days, could be human.

Presents of drinks and cigarettes helped. So did the convivial evenings enjoyed by the barber, the warrant officer, who had so many precious secrets in his head, and the two friendly Embassy men.

All Poles are devoted to their homeland, and many nostalgic thoughts and memories must have drifted through the mind of Warrant Officer Zaremba, as the drink flowed, and the air grew thick with smoke, and the conversation was doubtless deftly turned by the Polish visitors to familiar places and scenes, and Polish food, and Polish customs – and distant friends and relations.

It would be nice to see it all again – just for a short while, thought Zaremba.

Why not, they asked, why not go home on a visit?

But what about a passport? Well, they could probably persuade the Embassy to supply one. They might even persuade the Embassy to help in various other ways.

Things have changed, they insisted. And, after all, friends must help each other. No good being in the Embassy if you can't help a pal now and again, is there?

Both to Zaremba and also, without doubt, to the Polish spies, it all seemed too good to be true.

It was.

As in the case of Nikolai and the Three War Office Clerks something went wrong.

The operation came within an ace of success. It would have succeeded completely but for the alertness of certain RAF officers who had been concerned about the friendship between Gorski, Zaremba and the two Polish visitors.

Gorski and Zaremba were interrogated.

The dangers were explained.

Zaremba never went to Poland. He didn't want to, now.

Landing in Poland with a Polish passport, with no claim to any other status than that of Polish citizen from the moment he set foot in that country, he would soon have been faced with a very simple question:

'*Tell us everything you know, whether you want to or not. And if you don't want to, think again – or else.*'

Lucky Zaremba.

Beyond The Frontiers
On the whole, guile, patience, and enticement are employed by enemy Intelligence Services operating in Britain and the Western world when recruiting agents. Defects of character are sought, venality, idealism, and innocence are exploited, together with deep-seated emotions such as fear, greed, sex, and panic caused by unexpected and difficult financial circumstances.

However distasteful such methods may seem, they are clever, delicate, and gentlemanly compared with those which have been used against certain British citizens who were actually behind the Iron Curtain, particularly in Russia. Let us, then, watch the Russian Intelligence Service at work on its own ground.

Here we will see it in its most crude, brutal, and sordid form.

Here we will see blackmailers at work, unashamed, unabashed, and inhuman.

Case No.1

Claude Robinson was a man who like the Russians, and may still do so, though in view of what happened to him in Moscow his liking is now doubtless mingled with certain reservations.

He was particularly interested in promoting student group exchanges between this country and the Soviet Union, and in the fullness of time found himself being entertained one evening by some Russian acquaintances, at the Restaurant Moskva, in the Soviet capital.

There is an old Russian custom which calls for frequent individual toasts across the table. There is a further rigid custom connected with the custom: vodka glasses must be emptied at gulp.

Claude gulped a great deal.

When he was semi-conscious he was helped to a bedroom. He was undressed. He was subjected to a homosexual assault. The incident was photographed.

The whole thing was absurdly easy for the experts in blackmail.

There is no doubt that when he was later shown the photographs, the aim was to convince him that it would be wise to agree to any Russian Intelligence suggestions put to him later.

The implied threat was a criminal prosecution, and, among other things, the end of the hobby he was so interested in – cultural work among young people.

Claude Robinson did the sensible thing. He went to the British Embassy, and his early return to Britain was promptly arranged. But why was Claude Robinson chosen, with his harmless interest in culture and student groups?

Surely even the Russians were not interested in the secrets of British culture?

They were not.

They were interested in the students who made up the groups. Claude Robinson would have been recruited as a talent spotter, to identify students who – perhaps if they later became Civil Servants or scientists – might possibly respond to Russian advances.

His role would not have been dramatic or spectacular. But it would have been important. He might have been able to point to a future Fuchs, or Nunn May, or Vassall.

The problem raised is a difficult one.

It is impossible to tell a young man on a cultural exchange visit that he must decline all hospitality, even when it is offered in a public restaurant.

The Russians get round it by usually moving in groups of three or four.

The only other real defence is (a) knowledge of what may happen, and (b) knowledge of what to do if it does happen.

Case No. 2

James Ford is of interest because the Russians had to try three different baits before they trapped him.

Ford was a newspaper correspondent in Berlin, and in Berlin, in due course, a Russian official came quietly to him one day and offered him generous and tempting payment for copies of the agency services messages.

The argument was doubtless plausible enough. What harm in letting them see material destined in any case for publication? Nothing secret. No risk to James Ford. Just good money for easy work.

But the Russians knew that such communications often contain background material which for security, patriotic or other reasons never see the light of day in a newspaper. James Ford knew this, too, of course.

He firmly refused the offer.

He refused it at first in Moscow, also, where he was posted later, though there the bait was different.

It first appeared in the form of two attractive young ladies. They had no appeal to him.

Perhaps the Russians had not done there homework properly, or perhaps the delving into his past life had only now been completed. At any rate, they tried a third time, with a still different enticement.

This time they succeeded.

A hidden camera provided the necessary evidence of a homosexual relationship with a Russian.

James Ford listened to the blackmail threat which inevitably was produced.

Claude Robinson could claim that he had been the victim of a frame–up. For James Ford it was different. He had acted voluntarily.

It must have required clear thinking and considerable moral courage to do what he did.

Like Robinson, he went to the Embassy and told the story. A return to England was the only solution.

It was embarrassing, it was humiliating. But he at least saved himself from espionage, and consequences worse than a return home from Moscow.

Case No. 3

Frank Williams's case was quite different. He, most certainly, was a target worth aiming at. He was security guard to the Queen's Messenger, no less, who carried the diplomatic bag, with its secrets, between Moscow and Berlin.

No target in Intelligence, provided the potential gains are sufficient, is dismissed as impossible by the Russians and their allies, and in this case the contents of the bag carried by the Queen's Messenger was a prize worthy of a major effort.

All they needed was possession of the bag for a comparatively short time, because to properly equipped experts the opening of a diplomatic bag and the photographing of the contents presents no insuperable difficulties.

For a long time the agents of the Russian Intelligence

Service discreetly observed the routine followed by the Queen's Messenger and his guard on their journeys to and from Moscow and Berlin.

Finally they pin-pointed a time and place which offered the opportunities they sought. It was during a halt at an airport.

Here, all things being well, it might be possible to spirit the real bag away and substitute for a while with a facsimile one.

The operation could be done not once but perhaps every time a journey was made. The reward would be a golden harvest in the form of continuous Intelligence.

The secret observations revealed that the only snag in the way was Frank Williams.

Frank Williams had to agree to look the other way for a few seconds.

Some considerable time was spent by the Russians in observing the habits of the stalwart Frank Williams and trying to assess his character.

It was all most disappointing.

Frank was clearly a man who was very loyal to his country. Worse, he had no obvious vices to exploit.

Then, when the problem seemed to baffling to be solved, a minor piece of information came to hand.

Frank Williams's Error
Many people, quite ordinary people, such as tourists, think the Customs are fair game, a mildly exciting challenge to their nerve and ingenuity.

Frank Williams was one of them.

During his round trips he had sometimes indulged in some petty smuggling. For one thing, it probably relieved the tedium. It never amounted to much, hardly enough for a prosecution, certainly not enough for blackmail.

But it provided the key which the Russians were seeking.

One day in Moscow Frank Williams received a telephone call from a man with an American accent. No, said the voice, they had never met, but he had often seen Mr. Williams and knew that he regularly went to Berlin. Could Mr. Williams possibly take some German films to Berlin for developing and

Communist Intelligence services are constantly trying to penetrate Britain's security screen to get at national secrets. Typical of this ceaesless campaign were the activities of Gordon Lonsdale, a Russian, whose real name is Conon Trofimovitch Molody. This 'illegal' spy master controlled two spies in the Admiralty Underwater Detection Establishment at Portland, Harry Houghton and Ethel Gee. Also in his network were the American Communists, Peter and Helen Kroger, whose real name was Cohen. No passer-by wauld have suspected that their bungalow was a centre of espionage. Yet security men discovered otherwise.

Probing the rubble beneath the kitchen floorboards, they located a secret cache (right) containing Polythene-wrapped radio and other equipment. In a plastic shopping-bag was a wireless transceiver fitted with a single earpiece (below).

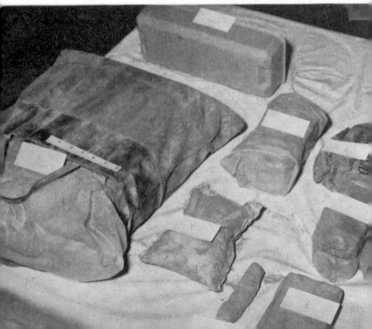

With the transceiver were two identical photographic prints giving a series of settings for the controls of the equipment against a series of three-figure numbers. This indicated that the equipment had been calibrated to transmit and receive at certain frequencies accordinig to the three-figure number selected (above). In one of the packages was a tape-sender (seen in the foreground) using magnetic tape for high speed transmission of short messages. In other parts of the bungalow were found many other devices of the spy, including this cypher pad (below) which was used in the coding and decoding of messages.

Plugged into the back of a radiogram in the living-room was as aerial which, leading through the ceiling, was stapled round the sides of the loft. A switch cut out the loudspeaker when it was used as an external loudspeaker. This fitting, incidentally, was similar to one found on the wireless in Lonsdale's London flat. A pair of headphones, normally hidden behind the radiogram, were plugged into a pair of terminals to which a tape recorder found in Kroger's study could also be connected. The equipment was capable of receiving and recording messages, sent by voice or Morse code, from anywhere in the world.

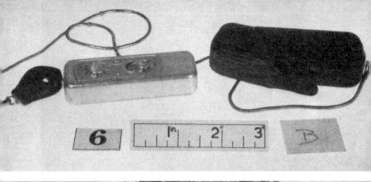

The cache under the kitchen floor also revealed – apart from six thousand American dollars, two lenses which could have been used for making microdots, and other items – a minature camera (above) and a casette with twelve frames exposed and two reloads. In the second drawer of the kitchen unit (below) was a plastic container holding magnetic iron oxide powder used as a visual aid to reading Morse signals recorded on magnetic tape. Other chemicals, plus photographic equipment, were found in the loft.

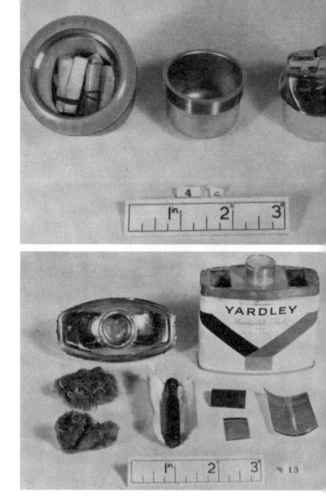

A table lighter (above) in the living-room had a secret hiding place similar to one found in Lonsdale's flat. It contained a one-rime pad with red printing partially used, two complate miniature pads with black printing, a miniature negative and two miniature prints of wireless transmission schedules.
The top of a talcum tin in the bathroom unscrewed, revealing two secret compartments. One of these contained a microdot reader (below). Fittings in the bathroom showed that in was used as a photographic dark-room.

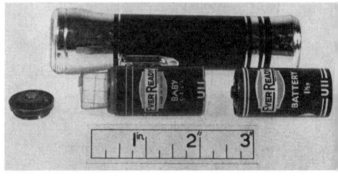

*An innocent-looking box of matches (top), owned by Houghton,
had a false bottom and was used as a hiding place.
The note illustrated refers to arrangements for Houghton's
meetings with a Russian Intelligence officer. The hip flask
with two secret hiding places containing magnetic iron oxide
powder(centre) was found in the Kroger's bungalow. The
electric torch (bottom) with two battery cells, one of which was
hollow, was in Lonsdale's flat and is identical with one found in
in the Krogers' bedroom.*

Lonsdale's flat also proved to be a mine of espionage gadgets, including this Chinese scroll which hung over his bed. The bottom roller was a hollow metal tube and contained a quantity of American dollar bills.

printing? Could they perhaps meet? Could Mr. Williams call at his flat?

He could and he did.

Frank Williams was suspicious. When he arrived at the flat the general atmosphere and refreshments did not seem American.

But the opening conversation was innocent enough, and the man had a bundle of American ten-dollar bills which looked genuine. He even counted them and asked Frank Williams to check the total.

Frank obliged.

Perhaps he was wrong, he now thought. Perhaps the man was an American after all. Some Americans take pleasure in living like the indigenous population.

Frank Williams discovered he had not been wrong when the man dropped the 'American' mask and offered him a straight payment of 10,000 dollars to co-operate in the matter of the Queen's messenger and the bag.

The threat came when Frank Williams indignantly refused.

Petty smuggling was one thing, it was pointed out. Currency smuggling was very different indeed. It was a very serious offence, under Russian law.

Frank Williams had clearly been smuggling American currency. He had the opportunity and he had smuggled other things, hadn't he? Furthermore, they now had a photograph of him holding dollar bills to prove it. They had just taken one.

Frank Williams said he must think it over, though he had no intention of submitting. He reported the position.

So, once again, the British Embassy had to listen to a story of attempted blackmail, and once again a British subject had to be removed from the city.

The attempt at recruitment was a failure, so the story can be told.

There are other cases where Russian blackmail succeeded, but the spy was caught.

There must be still others where the Moscow men have

trapped their victims and still hold them, stories known obly to the Centre – and to its victims.

Dot-Dash-Dot Men

Inevitably, such people as wireless operators in our embassies are regarded with a speculative eye by hostile Intelligence Services, for they possess important information such as call-signs and frequencies.

No Russian Intelligence officer worth his Siberian salt could do other than regard an operator in the British Diplomatic Wireless Service as a target worthy of the greatest effort.

One operator and his wife were drawn into social relationships with other Russians by an apparently harmless Russian occupying a non-confidential post in our Moscow Embassy.

The good-natured British couple, perhaps conscious of the hospitality they were receiving, gave presents of clothing and other articles from Britain to their Russian 'friends'.

This was fair enough. The trouble, and it could have been serious, arose when little by little the couple began to use such articles as a form of currency payment.

The Black Market blackmail trap was ready to be sprung. In due course it was.

But again the victim did not submit. He explained his situation to the Embassy and, once again, there was an issue of one-way tickets from Moscow.

Ill-Met in Wandsworth

The above cases have shown a heartening resistance to blackmail. The story of a young wireless operator called Henry Nicholls is different.

No blackmail for Nicholls

To this day it is not known for certain why Nicholls became a Soviet agent.

The story is simple. The background more interesting.

One day in April 1952, a Soviet Embassy official, known to be a spy, set out to keep an appointment.

As is usual with these people, he spent several hours trying to throw off anybody who might be observing his movements.

Eventually, in the respectable suburb of Kingston, London, he met his man. The man was Henry Nicholls. Nicholls produced papers. The Russian took notes.

You could almost say that they were old friends, because it is now known that they had met on at least six previous occasions.

But they were only destined to meet twice more, because on the second occasion, in St. George's Park, Wandsworth, they were arrested, and Nicholls was found to be carrying a wallet containing details in his own handwriting of call-signs, frequencies, and other important Diplomatic Wireless Service information.

The Russian was sent home,

The Briton got four years in prison. He was lucky.

In espionage, the difference between being a diplomat and not being a diplomat would seem to be an unpleasant sojourn in prison – in this country.

In some countries, the difference can be a bullet.

Why Did He Do It?

Henry Nicholls has never provided a satisfactory explanation. But perhaps if we look at his character and career we may find an inkling of the truth.

Nicholls joined the Diplomatic Wireless Service, after leaving the Army, in 1948. Two years later he was posted to Moscow.

There is no doubt that he was glad to go. For one thing, it seems likely that he was already interested in Communism, and now he would be able to see it in action. He arrived in Russia enthusiastic for the adventure.

In Moscow, two things happened.

On the one hand, he was impressed by the efforts and ideals of the Russian people. In some ways, no doubt, his earlier interest in Communism had already conditioned him to be thus impressed.

On the other hand, he was a misfit in the Embassy. He could not enter into the very restricted British society available to him.

He was too introspective. He was too unsociable.

Moody, isolated by his own nature, and unhappy, his work deteriorated even to the point where a transfer was considered. Being young, criticism of his work doubtless led to further resentment.

He was indeed ripe fruit for the Russian Intelligence Service.

Perhaps he was recruited during one of the frequent visits to Russian cinemas which became his outlet, or, perhaps, and quite possibly, by one of the Russian women on the Embassy domestic staff. It is significant that he disappeared from the Embassy for most of the day when he was due to leave. Maybe he was saying a fond farewell, but maybe other things were said in addition.

Sometime, somewhere, during his year's tour of duty, Henry Nicholls became a spy for Russia.

Perhaps he did it for ideological reasons, or because he had a social chip on his shoulder. Maybe because the Russians really seemed to appreciate him, as well they might, while his own countrymen did not, and it seems hard to blame them.

Possibly the explanation is even simpler.

It almost looks as if Henry Nicholl's dark, inhibited, and unfriendly nature had provided him with a ready-made, built-in, do-it-yourself spy mentality.

How do we stand?

We have seen how the hostile spy machine is organised and we have watched it at work.

The assessment must be that it is subtle and brutal, as occasion demands, that it is of vast dimensions, and that its agents delve in wide and varied fields.

Now let us glance briefly at the other side of the picture.

Like all large and ruthless organisations it has its weaknesses.

There is no doubt that Russia expects results, and in the attempt to achieve them, especially in the recruitment of new agents, some of her talent spotters go astray.

Ordinary courtesies shown to a Soviet official, or an interest, real or politely simulated, in Russian art or literature, or in conditions in the Soviet Union, are all noted. Often the individual concerned, apparently for this reason alone, thereupon begins to figure in the records as a potential recruit or 'unconscious' informant.

Here are typical messages between Moscow and Canberra. They were included in the report of the Australian judicial inquiry produced after the Russian Intelligence officer, Petrov, had defected and revealed all that he knew.

In the Australian report the judges clearly explained that many examples were found in the Petrov papers of the making down for 'study' of persons whose patriotism no one could question.

These messages give good indications of the line of thought pursued by the MVD, as it was then called, and seem to show either an inordinate degree of wishful thinking by Moscow Centre, or an over-anxious desire to please on the part of the operators in the field:

' Jack Hook, the president of the Sydney Trade Union of the Labour Council, labour supporter, one of the leading members of the Labour Party. Collaborates with the Communist Party. Holds progressive views. "K" considers H to be a man who deserves to be trusted' (p. 152).

The symbol 'K' stands for the Australian talent spotter

who recommended Hook to the MVD. Though obviously anxious to please his Russian masters his accuracy left much to be desired since the Royal Commission were able to satisfy themselves not only that Hook was positively anti-Communist but also that he did not even know 'K'.

'Concerning McLean. In the political Intelligence Department of External Affairs of Australia there works, with the rank of First Secretary, F. J. McLean . . .

'According to Sadovnikov's description, McLean has access to secret documents, knows well many workers in the Department of External Affairs, attends diplomatic receptions and consorts with members of the diplomatic corps.

'He treated our representatives in Camberra with respect, willingly accepted invitations, and attended receptions arranged by our diplomats in private apartments.

'During discussions he expressed dissatisfaction with the Menzies Government. . . . Furthermore, he is more talkative and frank when he is at a small gathering or at private receptions. . . .

'One of our trustworthy agents . . . considers that he could supply valuable information . . . should be skilfully and tactfully handled and be convinced that nothing that he will say will come to the knowledge of any Australians. . . . It should also be taken into account that McClean has a large family and is badly off materially. . . .' (pp.157-8)

Petrov never carried out this instruction because he discovered that McLean was in hospital, and likely to remain there for some time. But casual acceptance of slight hospitality, coupled with the financial problem of bringing up a large family, had proved sufficient to bring McLean within the talent-spotters' sights.

This type of miscalculation was not peculiar to the operations in Australia. It was also specifically noted in the Report of the Royal Commission on Espionage in Canada, produced after the Russian cipher clerk, Gouzenko, had defected.

In the documentary evidence appeared the name of a colonel in the Canadian Army whom the Russians regarded as a subject for study with the ultimate object of recruitment. In his evidence – which the judges accepted without any reservation – this colonel state:

'They have misinterpreted our sincere endeavour, both my wife's and mine, to make them feel at home in Canada, and to show them something of Canadian life; but I am cured' p.52).

Perhaps the Centre puts too much pressure on her agents in the field, drives them hard, threatens them too much.

The result, whatever the cause, is that much work and money is expended to no purpose whatever.

Even so, the fact remains that the Russians and their allies are forever on the look-out, forever probing and testing. And lest we take too much comfort from the above examples, let us note one more message from Moscow to Canberra:

'Concerning O'Sullivan in reply to your paragraph. . . . We regard the study of O'Sullivan as very full of promise. . . . It is essential to verify the data supplied by O'Sullivan about himself. . . . A verification is being carried out by us in England; we shall inform you of the outcome.

'In order not to draw the attention of the counter-intelligence. . . O'Sullivan should not be invited any more to the Embassy. . .

'It is desirable that, when a suitable opportunity offers, you should ask him to compile for us a survey concerning the economic, political, and military penetration of Australia by America, with the inclusion of unofficial data. Warn O'Sullivan that his survey will not be published . . . and that it is required by you for your personal use. Promise him that the time spent . . . will be compensated by you. . . .

'We request you to inform us in detail in every letter concerning progress in the study and cultivation of O'Sullivan' (pp.199-200).

In fact, Petrov did cultivate O'Sullivan a little further and the case might have held much promise since, in the following year, O'Sullivan was appointed Press Secretary to the leader of the Opposition.

Before the date of this instruction O'Sullivan had, indeed, already supplied to the Russians a report on 45 other journalists. The Australian authorities accepted this report as authentic but withheld it from the published evidence because of its scandalous nature.

It represented a major contribution in talent spotting.

There are other weaknesses in addition to those noted in the field of talent spotting.

One is the mania of the Moscow Centre to supervise the most minute detail from the distant Russian capital.

We have already observed that even street meeting places, dates, times, and other details are rigorously controlled from the Centre. It is inevitable that such remote control should lead to delays, queries, counter-queries, and, in the event of a sudden and necessary alteration of plans, to confusion, mistakes, and dismay.

A second weakness is almost unavoidable in such a large, monolithic, heavily disciplined organisation. There are bound to be frail human links, or links which were strong when they started but which have weakened with the years and the labour.

Human nature is flexible, human characters do not remain static. They are constantly changing for the better or the worse.

Even people in the Intelligence Services of Russia and her allies are subject to emotions such as fear, resentment, greed, spite, an excess of strain, or a political conversion.

Then one of the weak links may snap.

Then there is a defector to the West, and the balloon goes up.

Added to the efforts of our security authorities, the information brought over by a defector can be inestimable value to the West and disastrous to our opponents. There have been quite a few.

Doubtless there will be more.

Finally, the spy has also to contend with the vigilance of our own population.

Despite certain lapses over the years the British people are a highly observant, suspicious, intelligent, and patriotic race.

No spy is safe.

The Odds Against
The spy may listen to the comforting words of his spy master. He may soothe his nerves with recollections of the elaborate precautions taken to protect him, and flatter himself upon his guile.

He may elude for a period the attentions of the Security authorities and his fellow citizens, since no spy can be caught until he had done some spying.

Yet in the long run the odds are against him. For one thing, despite all the precautions, the cunning, and the ingenuity, he cannot protect himself against the weak link: the defector in his own organisation.

There is nothing whatever he can do about that.

He can smother his conscience. He can enjoy his money. But he is not, never will be, and never can be – safe.

Nevertheless, he can do a formidable amount of damage before he is caught.

How not to become a spy
(In six not-so-easy lessons)

1 If you find yourself in touch with an Iron Curtain official, mention the matter to a superior officer or your industrial or departmental Security officer. He will give you advice, and you may be able to continue the association if you so wish. Keep him informed all the time. It costs nothing, and is easy.

2 If you become friendly with a foreigner, especially and Iron Curtain diplomat, ask yourself two questions:

(a) Is he really seeking friendship – or information?

(b) Why should he choose *me* in order to learn, for example, about 'the British way of life'?

3 Avoid performing any paid service, however innocent it may seem, for an Iron Curtain official. It could be the beginning of the end of you.

4 If you are already, innocently enough, friendly with any of these people and have not reported the matter, safeguard yourself by doing so at once. Your forgetfulness will doubtless be overlooked, this time.

5 If you are abroad, behind the Iron Curtain, remember that you may be led into a trap and blackmailed. Do not make the mistake of thinking that you could be of no use to an enemy Intelligence Service. You might be.

6 If you are in an Embassy behind the Iron Curtain, remember that you will almost certainly be assessed as a potential recruit, willing or unwilling. Try to live sensibly and soberly, and not become too isolated from the British community. But if anything goes wrong – tell the Embassy. It will not surprise them. They've heard it so often before.

How to become a spy
(In six easy lessons)

1 Let it be known to your friends, casual acquaintances, and strangers that you have secret information, or are in a job where you may be able to obtain it one day.

This would attract treasonable propositions or threats, which may or may not be possible to resist.

2 Think you are cleverer than you are. Be conceited. Tell yourself that you are fully capable of handling any regular association with Iron Curtain officials without informing your superior officer or local Security officer.

If the Iron Curtain man is a diplomat, convince yourself that it's only your fascinating personality, wit, and friendship that attracts him. If you can believe that, you can believe anything. You're on your way.

3 Develop a few vices, especially abroad, so that with luck you can be compromised and blackmailed.

4 If you cannot manage a vice or two, just be foolish, with the same end in view. If you can't be foolish, be incautious.

5 Accept favours and hospitality from Iron Curtain officials, so that you put yourself under an obligation to them. When, in return, they ask some harmless service in exchange for good money, accept at once. This encourages them, and, if you pursue the matter to a logical conclusion, you should land yourself safely in prison one day.

6 If you do not fancy prison, especially in cold weather, persuade yourself that if you become a spy you will never get caught. You will, of course, in the end, but one must not start with a defeatist attitude.

Security Defences

Since the threat of espionage is very grave and quite a lot is known about the way spies are recruited and operated it is common sense to take steps to make spying more difficult and more dangerous. This is what security is about and it's objects are:

(a) to prevent anyone having access to secrets who is not authorised to see them;

(b) to ensure that everyone who is authorised to have access to secrets is trustworthy, disciplined, and alert; and

(c) by the application of the 'need to know' principle and in other ways to minimise the damage a spy can do if he gets inside the defences, to maximise the risks he has to run and to facilitate his detection when suspicion has been aroused.

Physical (which includes document) security may sound dull, but it is a matter of vital importance. The following passages give some advice on how you can help to achieve it. They are worth reading if only to refresh the mind.

Physical security, tiresome at first, can become a habit, which, once acquired, becomes as much part of daily routine as cleaning the teeth.

Some advice on:
How to foil a spy

1 *Read and observe your departmental security instructions conscientiously. They have been drafted by people who understand the threat of espionage and are designed to help fight it.*

2 Don't discuss classified information outside the office. Inside the office follow the 'need to know' principle. This is the rule that a particular piece of information is not passed on to a person who does not require it – even though such a person is authorised to handle secret information.

Apart from anything else, there is the chance that, since he does not deal with the subject himself, he may not appreciate its significance to a spy, or safeguard it with the same care as you do.

It should indeed be a matter of etiquette and good manners not to seek information to which you are not entitled. It places a colleague in the embarrassing position of either having to refuse you, or else break the rule.

3 Keep the office tidy. Office material may otherwise get hidden by other things.

4 Keep classified papers on your desk or table or in the appropriate container. Don't take classified papers to the canteens, lavatories, or cloakrooms.

5 Observe the rules about locking up at lunchtime and during short absences from the room.

6 Check that all classified material is put away securely at the end of the day.

7 Don't leave security keys where unauthorised people can get at them, even for a few seconds – a wax impression can be taken in a matter of moments.

8 Don't keep papers loose. Attach them as soon as you can to a file. Loose papers are meat to a spy, but papers which have been properly filed cannot be removed without leaving a gap in the file which may be noticed.

9 Avoid over classifying papers. When you have classified a document, ask yourself: 'Could I safely and sensibly give it a lower classification?' Too many papers to guard means that the important ones receive less attention than they should.

10 Don't take classified papers away from the office, even when you are travelling officially, unless it is strictly necessary and you know and have complied with the rules.

11 Don't discuss secrets on the telephone.

12 Do not use a telephone number, the date of a birthday, or any other obvious number, for the setting of any combination; and never write the combination in a diary – or in any other insecure place, even in code.

13 Take care of your pass. It is a valuable document.

14 See the windows and doors of the building are secure at the end of the day, if such is your responsibility. Burglaries by spies may not be frequent. But they can certainly happen.

15 Don't hesitate to ask the advice of your division, branch, section, or industrial security officer. Report to him anything you think may be of security interest. *It will be treated confidentially.*

Conclusion

Three things in particular are needed to protect our secrets from hostile Intelligence Services. They are:

INTEGRITY
COMMON SENSE
KNOWLEDGE

These will aid the defences of our way of life.

These will prevent national and personal tragedies.

It is when one or other is absent that the hostile Intelligence Service gets through to its target.

This booklet cannot enforce INTEGRITY and COMMON SENSE. It can only point out the consequences of a lack of them.

It has tried to provide some basic KNOWLEDGE.